THE ISLE OF AR

KEN HALL

Miss McKelvie's shop in Brodick (also visible in the lower picture on page 9) with Andrew McKelvie (her brother) and a shop assistant posing for the camera. Note all the postcards for sale in the right-hand window.

Royalties from the sale of this book will be donated to the Isle of Arran Heritage Museum.

Stenlake Publishing

2001

First published in the United Kingdom, 2001,
by Stenlake Publishing, 54–58 Mill Square,
Catrine, Ayrshire, KA5 6RD
01290 551122
www.stenlake.co.uk

Printed by Blissetts, Roslin Road, Acton, W3 8DH

ISBN 978 1 84033 635 1

ACKNOWLEDGEMENTS

I am grateful to Stuart Gough and Grace Small of the Isle of Arran Museum; Mr Robert Smith, formerly of Ashlar farm, Machrie; Mr Stewart Lambie and Grace Hamilton for the loan of early Brodick photographs; Mrs Janet Johnston and many more Arran friends for their help and support in putting this book together. Thanks are also due to Mrs Moira Cherrie of Rutherglen who offered the Dippin photographs taken by her grandfather, George Stewart, and whose collection is now housed in the Mitchell Library in Glasgow, to Robert Grieves, who supplied photographs of early Arran transport and buses, and to Oliver van Helden of Stenlake Publishing. Thanks to Ian Brodie for providing additional information about Arran steamers for the second edition of this book.

This second edition of *The Isle of Arran* has been published posthumously following Ken Hall's untimely death in 2003. Ken had a lifelong affinity with Arran, and in accordance with his wishes royalties from sales of the book will continue to be donated to the Isle of Arran Heritage Museum

This is an example of an early postal cover, and was sent on 13 September 1807 by R. Bauchop of Arran Castle to Mr Thomas Bauchop of Muirhouse, Mid Calder. The postmarks are a straight line ARRAN, a straight line SALTCOATS, and a script 7. In the late eighteenth century mail was taken to the mainland by 'Courier', which was probably the name of the ship which plied out of Lamlash during that period. Subsequently mail was carried between Brodick and Ardrossan, and in the 1830s the *Brodick* was the last sailing schooner to carry mails on this route. The first steamboat came down the Clyde in 1814, but it was not until 1872 when the iron pier was built at Brodick that these ships could land passengers, mail and stores at a pier. Hitherto, the ships had to anchor offshore and transfer everything to open ferry boats, from where goods were taken ashore to the boat slips. The regular use of steamboats began in 1828.

INTRODUCTION

Lying in the Firth of Clyde, the Isle of Arran is some twenty miles in length and twelve miles across at its greatest width. The distance round the island by road is some 56 miles. Two roads to the south traverse it, the String and Ross roads. The north is made up of hills and peaks, rising to the highest, Goat Fell, at 2,866 feet, while the south of the island contains flatter arable areas and moors. This geographical division gives Arran the name of 'Scotland in miniature'. There is plenty of evidence of early settlement, with artefacts and sites dating back to the neolithic and Bronze Ages.

Access to Arran is by ferry from Ardrossan to Brodick, a 50 minute journey. In summer a small car ferry also operates from Clonaig in Argyll to Lochranza, taking 30 minutes. The main activities on the island are farming, forestry and tourism, and in the summer the population of approximately 4,500 trebles with the influx of visitors. Other activities include a creamery making a Dunlop type of Arran cheese, craft shops and many other small businesses making products to tempt visitors, and also exporting their wares for sale on the mainland.

Deer roam amongst the hills in the north of the island, and since 1952 the Forestry Commission has planted a lot of the lower hills and moorland of the south, mainly with spruce and larch. Farmers finding it necessary to diversify their business activities have developed holiday accommodation on farms, along with pony trekking, farm parks and fish ponds as alternative sources of income.

Once on the island, visitors discover a tranquility and sense of friendliness. The villages do not change radically from year to year, and many families come back annually for holidays, and bring their children and grandchildren with them. Many people book up for their next year's stay as they leave, so it can sometimes be difficult for newcomers to find a slot during the busy summer months.

Most of the illustrations in this book are reproduced from postcards, a large number of which were produced from photographs taken in the 1890s. The cards themselves were sent to all parts of the world, 90% of them by people holidaying on the island. Messages, and even addresses, can prove to be most interesting. The number of postcards of Arran that have been produced is uncountable, and over the years more and more continue to come to light. Images of Lamlash and Brodick are numerous, and even Lochranza is well represented. The Steen series of the 1920s, featuring views around Lochranza, was numbered and runs to at least 57. Postcards produced by Valentine's are interesting as a checklist exists revealing the date of photographing according to the reference number on the cards. The earliest Valentine's cards date back to 1878.

This book is really complementary to my two previous postcard books on Arran, and is also laid out as a tour round the island, going anticlockwise and starting in Brodick. I hope that the pictures largely speak for themselves – the captions are intended to add some supplementary information, dates and explanations.

This early letterhead is one of a series of engravings of different views round Arran, printed by Banks & Co. of Edinburgh. Some artistic license is evident, with, for instance, the peak of Goat Fell shown to be unrealistically steep. The castle is in evidence on the far side of Brodick Bay, whilst the nearby large house is no doubt the Douglas Hotel.

The paddle steamer *Heather Bell* was built in 1871 and owned by the Duke of Hamilton's trustees. She was used on the Ardrossan–Arran run but despite being very powerful had to be taken out of service in the summer of 1871 for repairs. Alterations were made in May and June of 1872, and she returned to service when Arran's first pier (above) was opened at Brodick on 17 June 1872. She was sold early in 1874, as she was really too powerful a ship for the route, and her consumption of coal made her too expensive to run.

The first Brodick Fair took place in the early 1830s, and in the 1880s, when this picture was taken, it was being held at the pierhead. The main purpose of the fair was for stock trading, but it was an important social event too and stalls and entertainments drew crowds from the mainland as well as locally. Enthusiasm waned during the Second World War, after which the fair ceased. This George Washington Wilson photograph shows the steamer *Eagle* at the pier. She was used on the Broomielaw to Arran excursions.

Since the early days of the iron pier, there have been a great many changes to the structure of Brodick's pier and its ancillary buildings. A large wooden pier was built in the early 1900s, with further major work carried out in 1946 and again in 1957, when a purpose-built car ferry service started. The roll on - roll off facility became operational in 1976 when the vehicle causeway was completed. This picture shows the turbine steamer *Glen Sannox* at the pier.

The postmark on this card is 1911, so the warships in Brodick Bay must have been on exercise prior to the First World War. The picture also shows the heavy structure of the wooden pier, built to replace its iron predecessor. *Duchess of Argyll* lies alongside.

A typical Clyde puffer, the *Roman*, unloads coal onto a lorry while the steamer *Kildonan* occupies a berth at the pierhead in Brodick. The owner of the *Roman* was Alisdair Kelso of Corrie. This picture was taken in the 1950s. *Kildonan* provided a daily cargo service from Ardrossan to Brodick from 1949 (at which stage she was called *Arran*) until the arrival of the car ferry.

Another puffer, this time a 1960s shot of the *Lady Isle*, registered at Troon, about to depart from Brodick pier.

The old quay at Brodick is still evident today, below the bridge and burn outlet. The sails belong to a fishing smack.

Brodick old quay is used by small boats and cabin cruisers today.

The paddle steamer *Waverley* photographed on one of its regular summer visits to Arran in July 1996. Day trips currently run from Ayr, calling at Brodick en route to Loch Goil. Some passengers only go as far as Arran (where others can also join the ship). Trips also operate from upriver to Brodick and around Pladda.

The tennis courts, Brodick. In the 1950s and 1960s tennis was a very popular pastime, and many courts were refurbished in the early fifties. Today the game's popularity has waned, but a small number still enjoy the sport and compete for trophies established many years ago. New types of all-weather surface have replaced the old red blaes courts.

A 1930s beach scene at Brodick.

The road at Brodick pierhead in 1913, showing Miss McKelvie's shop beside Latona's fish market stall. These were ideally situated to catch customers coming to and from the ferry. A large row of bathing boxes can be seen at the opposite end of the bay.

148/130 Latona and the Shark at Brodick Pier

Cossimo Latona arrived in Arran in 1886 on an Italian barque which was shipwrecked on the island carrying a cargo of salt. He came from Palermo in Sicily, and married on 17 December 1894, aged 26. Initially he bought a derelict smack called the *Wemyss Castle*, which was stranded on the beach, and towed it up the burn where he lived in it as a houseboat. A hard-working man, he started out with a boat-hiring business, then began selling coal with a horse and cart, and later with a motor lorry. Eventually he built a house called Villa Latona at the end of Douglas Row in Brodick. He had a family of seven, with one of his daughters registered as being born in *Castle Wemyss*! The houseboat was destroyed by fire in 1897 on the day of the Brodick Fair, the same day as Queen Victoria's Silver Jubilee was being celebrated, and the disaster rather put a damper on the proceedings as far as local folk were concerned. One of Latona's sons formed the Arran Sea Transport Company, along with Willie Stewart and Donald Robertson of Blackwaterfoot, using puffers called the *Arran Rose* and *Arran Monarch*.
James Latona also owned the St Elmo Hotel, which was built in 1935, and part of which is now used as the ARCAS shop. In the advert for the hotel, visitors were asked to apply to the 'Proprietrix'. This was because the name Latona was not so well-known in those days, and it was thought that prospective customers may be put off by a foreign-sounding name. Cossimo Latona died in 1933. Unfortunately nothing is known about the story of 'Latona and the Shark'!

ST. ELMO PRIVATE HOTEL, BRODICK, ISLE OF ARRAN.

Hiring boats for rowing in the bay and fishing was quite a lucrative business in the summer months, as was the hire of bathing huts, seen here extending right along the beach. These were very handy to picnic in during cold wet weather if you had expected to spend a day on the beach and had nothing else planned.

A 1909 view of Invercloy in Brodick, with Brown's Smiddy on the right and Kames Cottage to the left. The new post office building now stands on the site of the smiddy. The large house up the hill was called Inchgarvie.

An earlier view of the same scene taken before some of the trees in the foreground were cut down and Inchgarvie was built. Note the cart on which a piano is being transported, steadied by a man standing next to it.

Another view taken from the same point, but this time looking the other way. The milk cart is passing Hunters Cottages and the joiners premises, now the site of the Brodick Bar. Goat Fell rises to the left of the picture. The milkman, John Currie, was known as 'Toorie' because of the bonnet or headgear that he always wore. He farmed at East Mayish, and milk from his large can was dispensed into smaller cans that were hung over gates or hedges, or left at doorsteps. Milk was sold by one or two pint measures, according to the regular orders, and payment was usually collected weekly, the cash often being left in the empty cans overnight.

Once the home of Lord Kelvin, the white house on the left was known as Castle View. Wooley's shop was next door. The roof and chimney of the post office, first occupied in 1886, appears across the road. This building became the golf clubhouse in 1913, and now houses a chemist's shop. The small wooden building with the white roof contained the shop started by the Misses M. & J. Currie in the late 1870s. They sold all sorts of small useful articles, not to mention landscape photographs taken by a Mr Beckett, a Pollokshields gentleman who made a profession of photography.

A 1923 scene at Invercloy, with Castle View and Wooley's on the left. M. & J. Currie's business flourished so much that in 1880 they built much more substantial premises, seen here on the right. The picture shows that there were once gardens in front of the houses; these have now been replaced by pavements.

Invercloy in the 1950s, by which time M. & J. Currie's shop had undergone further extensions and was being advertised as a 'High Class Grocers, Drapers, and General Merchants'. Having recently been taken over, the business is now an Alldays store. The shopfront to the left belonged to Alexanders, an ironmonger and general merchant's shop well-known for many years in Brodick. The shop opened in 1947, when Tom Alexander came back from the war.

The Cloy burn runs down secluded Glen Cloy at the north end of Brodick.

Mayish farm-steading is situated near the foot of Glen Cloy. In this picture oats are being cut by reaper. One man guides the pair of horses, while his mate sits on the reaper and operates the 'tilting board' using his foot. Corn gathers on the board, and when enough has been accumulated to form a sheaf he lets the board down and sweeps the bundle off with his 'tilting rake'. Later, the bundle is gathered into a sheaf using ties made from lengths of the straw. The sheaves are then 'stooked' in the field to dry and ripen.

This early tractor, a Fordston, was brought to Arran by Anderson's garage in Pirnmill. It was the first tractor on the island, and was used as a demonstrator round the farms. Here it is harvesting oats with a binder adapted to be pulled by tractor (normally it would have been drawn by three horses). It was a paraffin-fuelled vehicle with a water air cleaner. Jim Walker, from the garage, is on the tractor, which is pulling the estate binder in Glen Cloy. Later in its life the tractor was mounted on blocks in Anderson's garage and used to drive the electricity generator there.

Corriegills lies at the south end of Brodick on the hill called Dun Fionn. This hill separates Brodick from Lamlash to the south.

Auchrannie House Hotel in the Glen Cloy area north of Brodick was one of the more upmarket hotels on Arran, with prices ranging from 35 to 40 shillings per day in the late 1950s. Today the Auchrannie leisure and hotel complex is a far cry from the one house it used to be, and is one of the major hotel and timeshare complexes on the island.

A busy scene showing hay being loaded onto hay carts in the field. Prior to this it would have been cut and left to dry in the swath (the strip cut by the mower), before being collected in the field and built into hay ricks to further dry out and mature. Here the ricks are being loaded and carted into the farm-steading for storage in a barn, or in a large haystack. The hay would provide cattle fodder for the coming winter.

This card was postmarked with a Brodick double circle dated September 1903. It shows two girls 'tramping' the washing and two wringing out what look like blankets. These would have been hung out to dry, with the sheets laid out on the ground to bleach in the sun.

This farm is now part of the Isle of Arran Heritage Museum. Features include the old smiddy, a farm cottage with kitchen and bedroom displays, an archivists room, café and shop. Outside there are displays of old farm implements, tractors and other equipment. Practical demonstrations of horse-shoeing, sheep clipping, spinning and craftwork take place on regular special open days. Many interesting hours can be spent digging into Arran's past history at the museum, with very helpful and enthusiastic staff on hand to answer questions.

John Buchanan and George McIlwham give a piping display at the museum during one of its open days.

Donald Ferguson, previously the blacksmith at the Lakin smiddy in Shiskine, with Willie McKinley at the bellows, gives a horse-shoeing demonstration during an open day at the museum. It is wonderful to hear the ring of the hammer on the anvil, and see the red-hot iron being fashioned into the horseshoe shape, then smell the smoke as the hot shoe is tested on the horse's hoof for size and shape.

Brodick Castle lies in the shadow of Goat Fell and overlooks Brodick Bay to the south. Parts of the castle date from the fourteenth and sixteenth centuries. Now in the care of the National Trust for Scotland, the property once belonged to the Hamiltons, then the Grahams, and latterly the Montrose family. As well as the castle, its contents and the magnificent gardens, the Trust also administers 7,000 acres of mountainous country which includes Goat Fell and Glen Rosa.

The Old Quay (illustrated here) was a busy place when the main settlement of Brodick was situated on the north side of the bay. The Old Inn at Cladach accommodated visitors arriving from the quay; the latter became famous as the place at which King Edward VII and Queen Alexandra arrived in Scotland after their coronation on 20 August 1902. The quay was built on the instruction of parliamentary commissioners about 40 years after the inauguration of the packet service in 1770, at a time when the government was taking an interest in the development of the country by having roads and harbours built. It became the headquarters of the packet service, as well as the landing place when steamers began to ply regularly in the 1820s and 1830s. Brodick Old Quay is the datum point for the milestones which mark the perimeter of the island on the coastal road. It was around the quay that the original community of Brodick was gathered, but in 1844 when Anthony Archibald, the 11th Duke of Hamilton and 14th Duke of Arran married, the local population was moved bodily to new sites at Invercloy to provide the new owners of the castle with a greater degree of privacy. The old village was then demolished.

In 1933, this 20-seat Commer coach was purchased by North Arran Motors (E. K. Ribbeck and F. K. Newton). The bodywork was by John Stewart of Wishaw. The photograph was taken when the bus was new and still carrying its trade plates.

The quay at Corrie was built in 1882 to serve the sandstone quarry further south. It was also connected to a quarry above High Corrie beside the Coire nan Larach burn, where a very pure limestone was quarried. A tramline conveyed stone from there to the quay below. The red sandstone quarries had been abandoned by 1928.

The village of Corrie, approximately six miles along the coast road from Brodick, clings to the coast and lies in the shadow of Goat Fell. A second group of houses perched on the hillside above the village is called High Corrie.

Rock Cottage is situated at a very picturesque bend in the road. A war memorial stands on the rock beside it. In the 1970s the shop also housed the post office.

A sub post office was established in Corrie in 1853 and was located at the side of the inn, now a hotel. As with most sub post offices it was combined with a general store.

Like many others, the sub post office at Corrie was managed by the proprietor of the store, and usually changed hands along with the ownership of the shop. This picture shows Corrie Stores in 1978.

The village has a pure Gaelic name, *Coire*, signifying a cauldron, hollow, or a pool under a cataract. Corrie and neighbouring Glen Sannox were once prosperous crofting communities, but the Clearances of 1829 brought an end to their way of life.

Steamers hove to off Corrie to allow passengers to go ashore by ferry boat. With its two oarsmen, the ferry could take up to 35 passengers at a time, although those with heavy luggage or bicycles had to wait aboard and disembark at Brodick and then get a waggonette to transport them to Corrie.

The small port at Corrie berthed one or two fishing smacks. The *Betsy Crawford*, in port here, was often seen in Blackwaterfoot harbour as well.

The landing place always attracted a crowd when the steamer arrived offshore.

Duchess of Rothesay photographed at Corrie in 1923/24. Apart from occasional weekend runs, Corrie was not served from Ardrossan and instead calls were made by the cruise steamer from Gourock.

Duchess of Argyll lying offshore at Corrie. A very large number of passengers can be seen on her decks. Between 1919 and 1935 she was the regular vessel on the Gourock–Arran sailing.

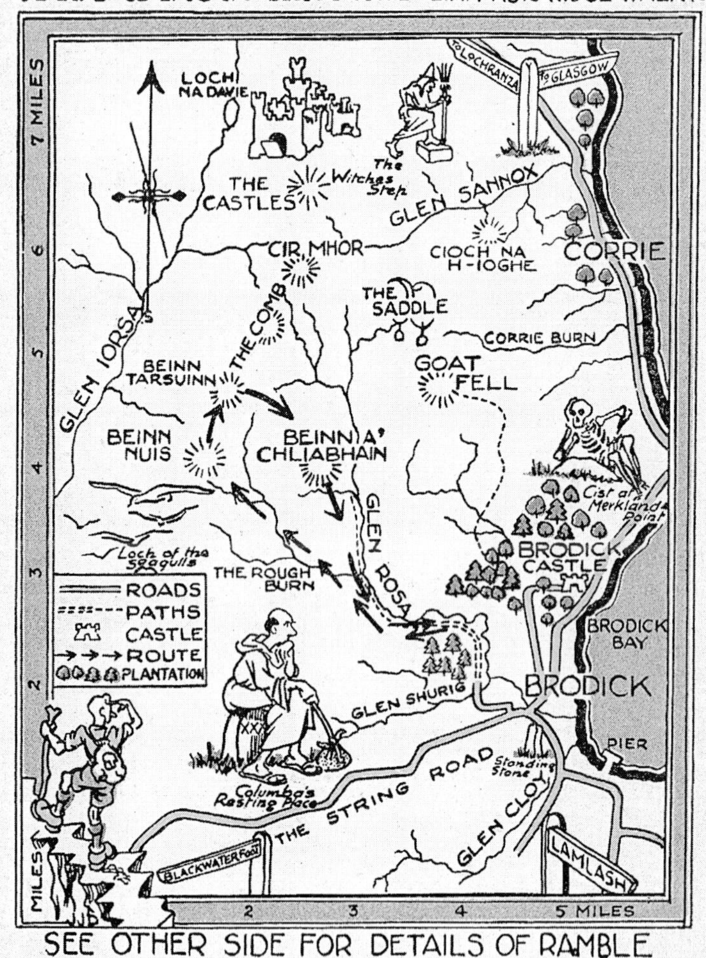

This is postcard no. 6 of Holmes' Tramping in Arran series which outlines various walks around the island. All are relevant even today. This one starts at Brodick pier and describes on the reverse a route by way of Glen Rosa and the Garbh Allt burn to the foot of Beinn Nuis. After a climb to the summit, the walk continues along the ridge to Beinn Tarsuinn, and from there back by Beinn a' Chliabhain and Glen Rosa to Brodick. The final instruction is 'to wear nailed boots on this excursion'!

Goat Fell is a very popular climb for people of all ages, and is accessible from paths around Brodick Castle, or from Corrie. The peak is 2,866 feet above sea level, and the only steep part of the climb is the final few hundred feet. National Trust rangers have recently repaired and improved the main path to minimise erosion damage. Goat Fell dominates Brodick Bay and the surrounding views from the summit on a clear day can stretch as far as Skiddaw in the Lake District, some 105 miles away. It is claimed that in all 122 peaks are visible.

The glen to the left of this view is Glen Rosa, whilst Glen Sannox is to the right; the ridge separating these two glens is known as The Saddle. The indent or 'V' shape in the faraway ridge is called the Witches Step. That ridge also forms the head, chest and profile of the Sleeping Warrior, as seen from the shores of north Ayrshire.

Cir Mhor is another rugged peak in the mountainous region of the north of the island. This view looks west over to the Kilbrannan Sound and the Kintyre peninsula. Beyond Kintyre, Islay and Jura can usually be seen, in particular the Paps of Jura. The view illustrates how barren the north of the island is, mostly comprising deer forest and contrasting greatly with the lowland terrain of the southern half of the island.

A houseboat in Glen Sannox. At one time such boats did not have to pay rent for mooring on the beach. Two pairs of tall white masts stand in the glen, quite a distance apart. These were used by ships on speed trial runs, and were part of the 'measured mile'. The point at which the first pair of masts appeared in line when viewed from the ship on the trial marked the start, and when the second pair appeared in line the vessel had completed a mile's journey. Today one can see the masts on the path to the Fallen Rocks although they are much more sophisticated now, with lights and other additions.

Sannox Bay, showing the coastal road before it turns westward and upward through North Glen Sannox. The old jetty was used to load barytes onto ships via the railway from the barytes mine. The main part of the railway consisted of a long balanced incline worked by gravity and a cable system. At the foot of the incline the track split into four lines which ran out on the level over two large concrete hoppers. From the underside of these, two tracks emerged to cross the Brodick–Lochranza road, and from there continued over a timber trestle bridge, an embankment, and onto the timber pier for loading barytes onto small ships. Haulage on the lower line was by horse and manpower. The wagons had a capacity of up to two tons.

Barytes is a heavy soft white mineral which was once milled and used as a substitute for white lead in paint. First mined in Sannox in 1840, nearly 5,000 tons were produced between 1853 and 1862. The mine was closed by the 11th Duke of Hamilton on the grounds that it 'spoiled the solemn grandeur of the scene'. After the First World War it was reopened, the railway was built, and by 1934 the output had risen to 9,000 tons. The vein ran out in 1938, however, and the light railway and pier were demolished after 1945. This photograph shows the mill house, where the mineral was ground (water from streams was used to power the mill). Trucks on the cable railway can be seen to the left, with the peak of Cir Mhor in the background.

The Fallen Rocks at Sannox were the result of landslips that left large conglomerate blocks of red sandstone piled up to a height of between 500 and 600 feet. It is said that these landslips occurred some 250 years ago, with 'a concussion that shook the earth' and that was felt in Bute and Argyllshire. The site is about three miles north of Sannox, and gives the impression of the end of a mountain range that has toppled over onto the shore. Huge rocky masses strew the steep slope, like an avalanche rushing down to the sea. Indeed some blocks are in the sea, and the path along the shore is well and truly blocked.

Situated on the western side of the island, Lochranza is Arran's most northerly settlement. On leaving Sannox the road climbs up North Glen Sannox to a height of 650 feet, then drops down the Boguille road and through Glen Chalmadale to reach Lochranza at sea level. This is a sea loch, and very noticeable when the tide is out. No road goes round the extreme northern tip of Arran, called the Cock of Arran, though a delightful walk can be taken by pathway and track.

A picture taken in Glen Chalmadale at the north end of the village. To the left, at the foot of the glen, is the site of the new Arran distillery. The buildings have been constructed in a very environmentally-sensitive manner, and with its visitor centre the distillery has become a major tourist attraction.

Located almost at sea level, Lochranza village is surrounded by hills on three sides. In 1836 Lord Teignmouth, author of *Sketches of The Coasts and Islands of Scotland*, wrote 'In point of gloomy grandeur no British bay surpasses Lochranza in Arran. Dark ridges hem it in, and an ancient castle, formerly an occasional residence of Scottish monarchs, occupies in the midst of it a central commanding position on a green projecting slip of land.'

The pier at Lochranza was opened in 1888 and steamers called there on their journeys between Campbeltown, Gourock and Glasgow. After 1946 the only passenger calls were made by the Gourock 'Duchesses', en route down the Kilbrannan Sound. The pier ceased to be used in 1970 but reopened in 2003 for calls by the *Waverley* and as an overnight shelter for the Kintyre ferry. As well as giving up travel tickets at the gangway, passengers also had to pay pier dues, as shown by the little box and gate at the pier entrance. Twopence was the charge for some time.

The entrance to the pierhead at Lochranza. The steamer lying alongside is the *Davaar*.

This picture shows the first TS *Queen Alexandra* (1902–11) at Lochranza pier. She caught fire in the Albert harbour dock at Greenock on 10 September 1911 and was replaced by a vessel of the same name which served on the Campbeltown route from 1912 to 1935.

RMS *Dalriada* tying up at the pier. *Dalriada* was built in 1926 and served on the Gourock–Lochranza–Campbeltown route from then until 1940. Judging by the number of people on the decks she was an extremely busy boat.

Appearing on a card postmarked 1926, this photograph must have been taken very soon after the *Dalriada* was built and came on to the route. Cars mix with horse-drawn gigs as they wait for disembarking passengers.

The *Duchess of Hamilton*, the second vessel bearing this name, was introduced in 1932 to replace the paddle steamer *Juno* on the Ayr excursion programme. She served on the Campbeltown route from 1946 to 1970.

Lochranza is a sea loch, and when the tide is out the appearance of the loch is completely altered. This 1913 photograph shows fishing skiffs at anchor in the bay. At high tide the castle is surrounded by water on three sides. It was once regarded as one of the 'royal castles' and is mentioned as 'a hunting seat of Scottish Kings in 1380'. The existing stonework dates from the sixteenth century.

A 1937 photograph taken looking south on the road past the pier. The view is over to Kintyre and the Argyll peninsula.

Lochranza pierhead in the 1930s. The rocks on the left mark the site of the new slipway which was built in 1972 in the shelter of the old pier. This is used by the small car ferry that operates between Clonaig and Lochranza.

The ferry and the mail that it brought was eagerly awaited, with the daily gossip exchanged by those that waited for it typified by the animated conversation of the group nearest the camera.

Lochranza post office in the late 1970s. Robert Kerr was postmaster at the time.

The Craw farm, perched 350 feet above sea level, looks north over Catacol Bay. Apart from some flat arable land at the head of Glen Catacol, there is little cultivated land between Lochranza and Pirnmill, as the ground rises steeply from the shore to the hills. Consequently there are few cattle, the farms being mainly stocked with sheep.

This row of houses is known as the Twelve Apostles. Situated on the shore at the head of Glen Catacol, it was built to house families displaced by the Clearances, during which tenants were moved off their holdings or crofts to make way for sheep farms. This took place in the mid-1860s. However the crofters could not be persuaded to use the houses, and preferred other parts or even emigration. The houses lay empty for two years before other tenants could be found.

An unusual view showing the back of the Twelve Apostles.

Below: Coming south from Catacol these cottages at Pirnmill sit on the coast with a raised beach behind them. They look over the Kilbrannan Sound to Carradale, with just the road separating them from a very pebbly beach.

Above: Catacol farm has some good flat arable ground around the steading, capable of producing winter fodder for cattle and also suitable for stock grazing. The glen stretches up into the hills following a picturesque burn southwards. This leads up to Loch Tanna, the largest loch on the island, situated at 1,051 feet above sea level. Above Loch Tanna tower the highest hills on the west coast of Arran, Beinn Bharrain at 2,345 feet, and Beinn Bhreac at 2,333 feet; these are Gaelic names for 'the hill with the little gap' and 'the dappled hill'. The view westwards from their summits includes the Mull of Kintyre, Loch Fyne, Islay and Jura. Eastwards the bare hills and deer forest over to Beinn Nuis and Goat Fell can be seen, while to the south the hills of Antrim in Northern Ireland are visible.

Very little evidence of the former nine hole Pirnmill golf course exists today. At the start of the Second World War in 1940, the course was ploughed up for agricultural use and never reopened afterwards. The point of the bay shown to the south of Pirnmill is known as Whitefarland.

This group of cottages at North Thunderguy beside Lennymore Farm lies in the shadow of Beinn Bharrain. Streams lead up to Corrie Lochan, which is situated almost 1,100 feet up the hillside and is enclosed by the shoulders of Beinn Bharrain; the walk up to it is very popular and not too strenuous. The name Lennymore means 'the great wet meadow'. The old form of Thunderguy was Tonregethy, meaning 'back to the wind'.

Altgolath at Pirnmill is still one of the larger farms in the area, using arable ground on the coastline as well as on the hill. Many families earned their living on farms in the old days, and they formed distinct small communities with clusters of homes to house the workers. This is of course quite different from today, when so much of the physical work is done by tractors and machinery rather than people and animals. The name of the farm is derived from Allt-gobhlach, meaning a forked stream.

Pirnmill centred around Anderson's store and post office. A stream flowed to the right of the store and provided the water power for Clark's mill, a building set back from the road where pirns were made out of local birchwood for the thread industry in Paisley. As well as having the post office, store and garage, Mr Anderson took photographs, many of which were made into postcards. The garage was sited behind the old smiddy, visible on the right of this picture.

This busy scene in front of Anderson's shop shows the point on the shore where the ferry and other small boats landed passengers and mail from the Greenock–Lochranza–Campbeltown steamers as they hove-to off shore.

The interior of the workshop at Robert Anderson's garage at Pirnmill. Mr Anderson had the Ford agency for the west coast of Scotland and supplied model T Fords which were built to order in Manchester. The chassis were then driven up to Airdrie where the appropriate bodies were built on – vans, lorries or saloon cars. The picture shows a model T engine block on the bench with its bearings being attended to. Leaning against the window is a trade plate – 0001 SJ – the first number issued for the County of Bute. Jim Walker, Duncan Kerr and Charlie Robertson are in the picture.

A scene at Immacher. The thatched cottage on the left is now the site of sheep pens beside the road and an enclosure where one can see ducks, hens and peacocks! The cottages and farm still stand beside a bad Z bend, just before the road dips steeply down to the shoreline.

The *Davaar* has stopped to meet the Pirnmill ferry boat whilst on her way to Lochranza after leaving Campbeltown. Built in 1885, she initially served on the excursion day trip from Greenock. In 1903 she was thoroughly overhauled and reboilered, and reappeared with only one funnel. When the *Kintyre* was run into and sunk in 1907, the *Davaar* changed in summer to the daily return service between Glasgow and Campbeltown, with the *Kinloch* operating in the other direction. On 14 March 1940 the *Davaar* finally brought this passenger service to an end; it had been running for over 114 years.

A 1960s view to the left of Anderson's shop. The Anvil Tearooms still exists today and is easily recognisable.

The message on this postcard, sent in 1911 by a holidaymaker to a friend in Manchester, says 'this is the house where Bowman stayed when he was here. Aunt Maggie and family are in the one on the right'. Whitefarland cottages sit beside the road as it leaves Pirnmill to climb up to Immacher. One feature very noticeable today are the palm trees in the garden beside the road that seem to flourish and have been there for over forty years.

McMillan's Temperance Hotel, Immachar. Temperance hotels were very common until the 1940s. This was rather an isolated location for a hotel with the nearest villages being Pirnmill to the north and Machrie to the south.

C. M. Weir's model T Ford grocer's van outside the Laggmore Boarding House.

Dougarie Lodge was built by the Duke of Hamilton in the mid-nineteenth century as a shooting lodge. It is situated back from the shore and boat house, beside the Iorsa River which runs up the glen to Loch Iorsa. The wooden bridge has since been replaced by a stone one. The blocks were used before a substantial bridge was built and when a ford was the main means of crossing the river. They are still used by fishermen and the more agile walkers. This photograph was taken in 1926, and the card it appears on is postmarked 31-8-39, just a week before the outbreak of the Second World War.

Behind Dougarie Lodge is a building which looks like the ruins of a castle, and attached to that are the kennels. During the last war, evacuees were housed in the kennel buildings for some time. This view was taken prior to 1907.

This card was postmarked at Machrie on 23 August 1935. At the time the village post office was run by Mr Sym, grocer, tobacconist and confectioner. He also hired out a car when occasion demanded. The first post office was established in Machrie in 1901 and was run by Mrs Weir, initially from her cottage. Mr Sym took over until 1954, followed by Mrs Hamilton until 1964. The post office was then attached to Ashlar farmhouse and was run by Mrs Mary Smith before finally closing on 8 October 1977. The message on the postcard reads: 'I am standing outside here although you cannot see me, P.'!

These standing stones are in the middle of Machrie Moor. Many monuments of the neolithic and Bronze Ages have been found in the vicinity, and owe their survival to the blanket peat covering the area. The moor encompasses a whole range of sites among which are chambered tombs, stone circles and hut circles, traditionally thought of respectively as funerary, ritual and domestic relics. A group of five closely-spaced stone circles lies beside the now unoccupied Moss farm buildings. The pleasant 1½ mile walk from the road is popular with visitors. Signs and information boards put up by Historic Scotland describe the artefacts and the history surrounding them, which dates back to between 3,500 and 4,000 BC.

A large peat stack being secured for winter fuel supplies. Jimmy Kelso of Torbeg, using some children for help, carts home peats cut on the Machrie Moor.

Kate McAlister of Torbeg farm watches hay being unloaded from hay wagons onto the large haystack.

On the left is the Lakin Smiddy which was run by the Ferguson family. James Ferguson was followed by his son Donald, who died in July 2000 aged 90. In the centre of the picture is the old Free Church building, which has since been demolished and a smaller more modern church building erected on the site.

Although a blacksmith to trade, Donald Ferguson, along with his father, also farmed the Lakin holding. He is seen here harvesting a crop of ripe oats with the horse-drawn binder. The three horses were named Nancy, Davie and Dora.

An interior view of the Lakin Smiddy. Holes are being punched in the horseshoe where nails will eventually secure it to the horse's hoof.

An early 1900s view of the old Lakin cottage with its thatched roof, taken before the more substantial sandstone house was built beside the smiddy.

The String road, photographed in the 1930s with Monyquil farm nestling below the contours of Beinn Nuis. The grocer's van is plying its trade from farm to farm.

A 1912 view of the tidy village of Shedog, with the Hamilton Arms Hotel tucked in to the left behind the large tree.

The Hamilton Arms Hotel with postman 'Cole' Currie on his horse brake, no doubt ready to journey across the String to Brodick with mail and passengers.

Hamilton Arms Inn,
Shiskin, Arran, 1876
M
To George Wooley,

Breakfasts,	4	
Luncheons,		
Dinners,		
Teas		
Suppers,		
Wine,		
Brandy,		
Whisky,		
Porter or Ale,		
Lemonade or Soda Water,		
Beds,	3	6
Attendance	1	6
Stabling	3	
Corn and Hay,		
	12	

Settled

This early invoice from the Hamilton Arms Hotel dates from 1876, when the proprietor was George Wooley. It was obviously a licensed premises, and not a temperance hotel. The items for 'stabling' and 'corn and hay' show that the traveller's horse would have been looked after too.

Prior to the arrival of motor buses on the island, horse-drawn brakes carried passengers to and from steamers arriving from the mainland. This one belonged to Colin Currie of Shedog, Shiskine who operated between Blackwaterfoot and Brodick across the String road.

Shiskine is really a continuation of a row of houses after Shedog on the road towards Blackwaterfoot. It is also the name given to the surrounding district. The store was just a few hundred yards along the road from Shedog, and in the 1920s the proprietor was A. McBride.

Further towards Blackwaterfoot, along from the store, is this group of houses, the nearest of which is Daisybank. The white cottage to the right of the tree was the police station, as denoted by a wee wooden sign to the left of the far away window.

During the 1940s and 1950s a long tin hut stood opposite the buildings in the upper picture. This was the village hall, where many a lively dance and concert took place. Latterly it became a shop and post office, the proprietor of which was E. Anderson.

Shiskine school, photographed in 1932 and showing the staff of two and their 55 pupils. Mr Angus Smith was headmaster and Miss Jean Gracie his assistant teacher. The schoolmaster's son Robert is in the middle of the front row of the group. Robert farmed at Ashlar farm in Machrie, and his wife Mary was the last postmistress at Machrie.

This card has a Shiskine postmark dated 30-8-09 and was posted by a resident at Sunnybrae, Blackwaterfoot. It bears the printed title 'Grannie at her Wheel'. The writer had been on holiday and was returning home having had friends over to stay in Arran. The message is typical and includes the usual weather report. One question remains, however: who was Grannie?

There is a small tidal harbour at the mouth of the Blackwaterfoot burn. The building surrounded by carts was the weigh house, where carts could have their loads weighed – those bearing hessian sacks probably contained wool from the sheep clipping. Coal, potatoes and other goods would all be weighed over the scales on arrival or departure at the harbour. The postmark is unclear but is from about the 1915 era. The card, sent to a Miss Cameron in Kilmarnock, states that the writer came via the steamer to Machrie and then travelled by bus to Blackwaterfoot for their holiday.

Carts gathered around a puffer, beached in the burn mouth, ready to unload a cargo of coal. It was quite a hard initial pull up the loose shingle for the horse with a full load on the cart. One puffer regularly seen here was the *Maisie*; another, owned by Charles Robertson and William Sym, was called the *Number Ten*.

A 1903 postcard showing a smack called the *Dasher* in the burn. The small house to the right of the bridge was the ferryman's cottage, which was built in 1886 along with the store situated beside the road. The building above the ferry cottage housed the stables for the nearby hotel. The farm to the right of the picture is now the site of the Kinloch Hotel.

The stone bridge at Blackwaterfoot replaced an earlier wooden structure. Until it was built, a ford further upstream took the heavier traffic.

A 1905 view with the *Dasher* of Ardrossan in the harbour with its sails furled. This was a typical fishing smack which went in pursuit of herring up the Kilbrannan Sound.

Another view of coal being loaded onto carts at the mouth of the Blackwater burn.

A horse and cart at the weighbridge. Note how the shafts of the cart have been uncoupled from the horse's harness so that the full weight of the cart and shafts is recorded as it stands on the weighing platform.

Fishing smacks lying at anchor off the mouth of the Blackwater burn.

The Drumadoon shore at Blackwaterfoot with the tide well out.

Gathering seaweed on the Drumadoon shore. This was carted to the fields where it was spread as fertiliser and ploughed into the ground. It was particularly useful for potato crops, being a valuable source of minerals, as well as nitrogen, phosphate and potash. As well as providing nutrients it also improved soil structure, which was useful as most fields near the shore had a high sand content. The seaweed was most abundant after heavy storms which washed it up above the tide line. These usually coincided with spring time, when the seaweed was applied before the land was ploughed and prepared for cropping.

The Kinloch Hotel in the 1950s, when it was under the care of Mrs Crawford. Still run as a family business today, the hotel has expanded greatly since then, having absorbed the adjacent Montana Hotel to become one of the bigger hotels on the island.

A mid-1950s view above the harbour, showing Miss Grieg's post office and shop tucked in beside the Kinloch Hotel. To the left up the hill is the bakery, grocers and large bank building. By this time virtually no commercial traffic used the harbour – today it is a haven for small boats, yachts, and lobster boats.

The golf course at Blackwaterfoot was established in 1896 and was part of the Shiskine Golf and Tennis Club. Originally it was on the shoreline on ground sub-let from Drumadoon farm. To start with it had nine holes, but it was extended to eighteen holes in 1913. Six of the holes were on ground quite high above the clubhouse, and in 1920 these were abandoned leading to the unique twelve hole course that it is today. The golf course has an idyllic setting with views up the west coast of Arran and over the Kilbrannan Sound and the Mull of Kintyre.

During the 1940s Drumadoon farm was comprised of some 70 arable acres and 580 acres of hill pasture, and carried a dairy herd of 34 milking cows. 20,000 gallons of milk were produced in 1948, and crops of hay, silage, oats, potatoes, turnips and kale were grown along with grass pasture. 145 hill ewes, 34 young cattle, 2 bulls and 4 horses were the other stock on the farm as well as 65 poultry around the steading. In the 1940s Drumadoon was a family farm under the guidance of Mr James Currie, and to help the family, land girls as well as students completed the labour force. These years were the beginning of the age of farm mechanisation. The Ford Ferguson tractor made a major contribution to working the farm, with tractors steadily replacing the horse at this time. The following photographs of life and work on the farm were taken by the author in 1950 and 1951 whilst he was an employee there.

In winter, cattle were all housed in byres and tied by the neck. They had to be hand fed in their troughs, and each day the 'grips' behind them had to be mucked out. The midden containing the farmyard manure was of limited capacity, so to store it as it accumulated the manure was pushed by barrow up ever-rising planks as the winter progressed. It became quite a balancing act as the planks were raised higher and higher on top of barrels and old ammunition boxes. However when it came to emptying the midden (by hand graip – there were no foreloaders in those days), it was an easier job to chuck the forkfuls down onto the trailer for spreading on the fields.

Horse ploughing was a very satisfying task, and an acre a day was a standard rate. A slow steady plod with a good team was best, with the earth falling neatly over in the furrow. Gulls and birds flew round about searching for worms, and the cry of the peewit was a lovely sound.

With the modern tractor and its three point linkage, a digger plough hitched on the back could plough a deeper furrow than a horse-drawn plough. This meant that odd stones and boulders were often hit, and these had to be taken out to avoid further damage to the machinery.

On Drumadoon farm, potatoes were grown for the stock seed trade – i.e. to produce potatoes which were sold for planting, rather than eating. Named varieties of seed were planted, then carefully 'rogued' to eliminate diseased or unhealthy plants. The plants were then inspected by officials and the crop certified. After this the crop was harvested, and the seed potatoes put into pits which were thatched with rushes and covered with earth for storage through the winter. The next spring they were 'dressed' by being put over a circular sieve and graded. Large ones ('tops') were removed along with the very small ones, called 'chats'. Stones and diseased tubers were also removed as they came over the elevator, and then the good seed was bagged, the bags sewn up and labelled and left ready for collection and sale. Varieties such as Arran Banner, Arran Peak, and Arran Pilot were grown on Drumadoon. These particular varieties were introduced by the work of Donald McKelvie of Lamlash, who received gold medals from the Royal Highland and Agricultural Society for his efforts on potatoes.

James Currie of Drumadoon photographed during a tea break while working at the potato pit. The 10 o'clock and 3 o'clock breaks were most welcome, and were sent out each day by the ladies in the farmhouse kitchen.

Sheep shearing in June first required the sheep to be gathered off the hill; they were then clipped by hand shears or machine. Ewes' fleeces had to be dry at the time, or the wool would spoil, so the operation was very weather dependant.

In winter the travelling mill came to the farm and spent a whole day threshing the corn sheaves. Neighbours from all round came to help. Sheaves were forked from the stack up to the mill men who fed them into the drum. Straw was bunched at one end of the mill and taken away to be stacked. Grain was bagged off at the other end and carried up to the granary. The dusty 'chaff' or husks were also bagged, to be used later for bedding. Threshing was a very social event as all the neighbours helped each other as the mill went round the district. The ladies of the farm all produced a magnificent midday meal, and as a result some of the milk cans in the dairy had a little less cream on the top of them than usual!

June and July was a busy time for hay, which was cut by a two horse reaper (left, shown in travelling position) and turned by a mechanical swath turner to dry (it was sometimes turned more than once). Later, when it was judged to be dry enough, the hay was raked into rows by a horse rake, collected from the rows by a hay collector (the 'tumbling tam') and made into ricks. These ricks matured in the field for a week or more, then were collected off the field by a horse-drawn rick lifter (a flat-bottomed cart) and either taken into the hay shed at the steading or built into very large haystacks.

Drumadoon was a progressive farm, not slow to adopt new farming methods, and in the 1940s, unlike many mainland farms, was already making silage. Grass was cut and immediately lifted from the field using the rick lifter. (Ken Hall and Jean Humphries – neé Currie, are seen on the job, below). The grass was then forked into a square concrete silo. Molasses was added from a watering can, the grass well tramped down, and the top sealed over and weighted down with large stones. In winter the silage was then fed to the cows. A bonus of making silage was that the women in the kitchen got hold of a little molasses from the barrel and made the most delicious treacle scones!

Oats were the main cereal crop in the 1940s, and after ploughing and harrowing the ground, seed was applied by the corn drill and later harrowed to cover it. At harvest time the field was 'opened up' by scythe to make way for the binder to cut the corn. Here Rev. James Currie (the son of James Currie) wields the scythe, while the rest make sheaves. The essential tea break was a chance for a chat and a gossip. Sheaves were stacked in sixes and left to dry out and ripen for two to three weeks. The crop was then 'led' into the stackyard and built into corn stacks.

Beside the fourth green of Blackwaterfoot golf course, and in the shadow of the Doon, stood a primitive thatched cottage belonging to Jimmy Neil 'the whelkman', and his wife Jenny. As well as gathering whelks off the rocks, Jimmy did occasional work on the golf course, collected rabbit skins, and helped unload coal boats when they came up the burn at Blackwaterfoot. The story goes that the men overfilled the buckets so that when they were swung over to tip into the carts, a little spillage occurred, leaving a coal harvest to be collected when the boat departed! The Neils had a donkey called Charlie and a garden in which they grew their own vegetables, their carrots in particular being the talk of the district. Water was drawn from a nearby well. Jenny collected whelks too, and when she had a full bag she left them at the side of the Drumadoon road for collection. She was paid 42 shillings per bag. Jimmy was a migrant ex-miner from Campbeltown, who arrived in his boat with Jenny, perhaps attracted by the small natural tidal harbour which can be seen beside the fifth tee on the golf course.

The Kings Caves are situated on a promontory between Machrie Bay and Blackwaterfoot, and are accessible on the Machrie side via a forestry path round the present forest on the north side of Tormore hill. From Blackwaterfoot the path leads from the golf course, below the Doon and along the shoreline below the raised beach of Drumadoon hill. The caves are reputed to have been a favourite resort of Bruce, and the largest is 100 feet long, 40 feet wide and nearly 50 feet high. Many relics, such as tusks of boars, deer antlers and bronze ornaments were found in its floor during excavations in 1909. There were interesting engravings and marks on the walls, but many have been defaced over the years, necessitating gates to protect the caves. New gates replaced the old ones six years ago, and were put in place by Historic Scotland. A large cave to the right was known as the 'Stables'.

The Shiskine valley is one of the most fertile areas of the south end of Arran, and some quite large farms once produced crops of hay, oats and potatoes, as well as grazing for mainly cattle stock, the sheep tending to be found on the surrounding hills and the less productive land. Large and medium sized dairy herds produced milk which was collected daily. From the 1950s, when the Scottish Milk Marketing Board gave stability to the dairy industry, the creamery at Kilmory processed this milk, mainly into cheese. Still being produced today, the Arran cheese is a very acceptable mild type of Dunlop cheese. Times change, however, and many dairy and beef cattle farms have converted to sheep farming, even on the low ground. This 1937 view shows Kilpatrick farm in the foreground, beside a field of oat stooks at harvest time.

Blackwaterfoot Bay, seen from the road leading south to Corriecraivie at the point known as Brownhead.

Whitefield boarding house at Sliddery was situated beside Whitefield farm-steading. From the 1900s the farmhouses were let out to summer visitors during the season, the families moving out to smaller abodes or even a barn for the summer months in order to earn valuable extra income from the visitors.

Kilmory post office *c.*1905. The village of Lagg is situated in a valley surrounded by trees, with a steep access road at either end. The post office really derives its name from the parish, rather than Lagg where it is located. A sub post office is still found in the shop at Kilmory.

A 1938 view of Lagg looking towards Lagg Hotel.

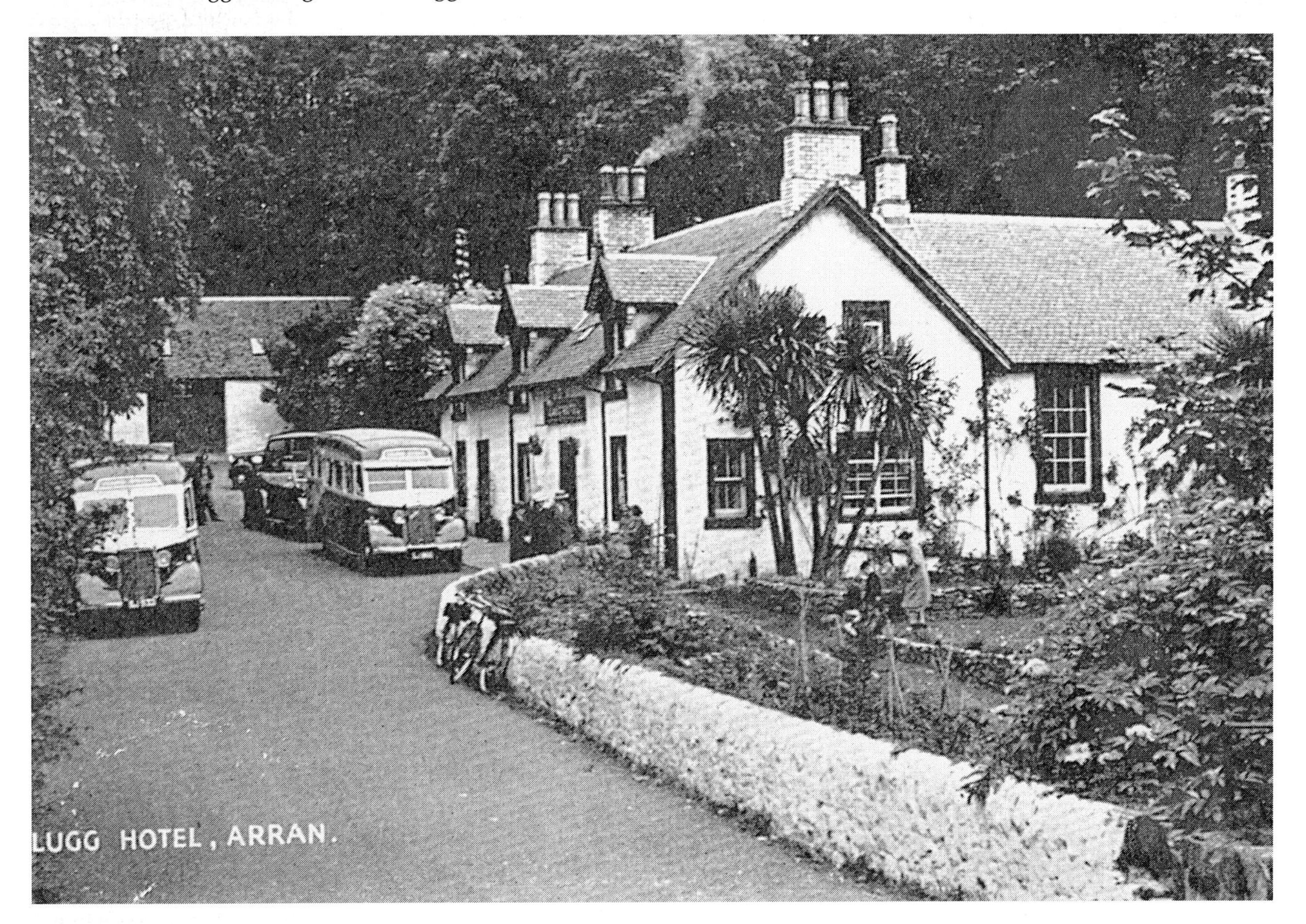

A group of E. K. Ribbeck's Bedford coaches pause for refreshment on Round-Arran tours at Lagg Hotel in the 1950s.

Due to the sheltered situation of Lagg, palm trees grow well and are a very distinctive feature round the hotel and its gardens.

After passing Bennan Head, the coast road drops down steeply to the port of Kildonan. This 1950s photograph shows the view over to Pladda and its lighthouse, with 'Paddy's Milestone' – Ailsa Craig – on the right horizon.

The Kildonan Hotel has a commanding view out to the Irish Sea and across the firth to the Ayrshire and Wigtownshire coast. It is reputed to be one of the oldest hotels on the island, and was in existence in 1800. This 1912 picture shows Kildonan Bay to the left.

A 1935 view of the hotel showing extensions on either side of the original building. All the island's hotels relied very much on summer visitors who would come for two to four weeks on their annual holidays with their family and friends. Until the 1970s very many came from the Glasgow area, with some from the east coast and others from England.

A fishing smack photographed in 1930 in the natural port of Kildonan, sheltered by a large outcrop of rock. The odd lobster boat still uses this anchorage today.

The coast road rises fairly high above sea as it travels over Bennan Head. Levencorrach farm is seen here, with the white gable end of Auchenhew House beyond.

Shannochie is a small group of houses beside the road between Kilmory and Bennan Head. Although facing north, they are really the most southern dwellings on the island.

A 1940s picture of the post office at Shannochie, one of the last in Scotland to have a thatched roof. The building is still there, but the roof has now been modernised.

On leaving Kildonan and heading north towards Whiting Bay one reaches Dippin, a scatter of a few houses and a large lodge. This 1909 card, bearing the printed caption 'At Dippen, Isle of Arran' poses several questions. Who are the two men and the lady? What are they carrying? Where are they bound for? Is this a flitting, old style? All the card says is June 1909, and on the address half, Florence E. Hadden, New York City.

George Stewart, a Glasgow headmaster, took many photographs at Dippin in the late nineteenth and early twentieth centuries. He was the grandfather of Mrs Moira Cherrie, who now resides in Rutherglen, Glasgow.

Mr Stewart is at the left in this picture, with Mrs Stewart to the right at the front of the group. All three ladies are holding knitting.

The cottages at Dippin, with sheets or blankets set out to dry and bleach in the sun.

An interesting study of children's dress in a typical middle class family.

The thatched cottage at Woodburn, Dippin, where George Stewart and his family spent many happy holidays with Miss Jane McKelvie.

The butcher's cart at Dippin, with Miss McKelvie holding a chicken, and Mrs Stewart (right) carrying another purchase. Peter Boa is wearing the typical butchers outfit.

Unloading a cartful of peats. These would eventually be built into a tidy peat stack to secure a supply of fuel for the winter.

A group of children and adults, some of whom are seated on peat barrows. Were the hats designed to provide protection from the sun, or were they just for adornment? Nurse and baby are not wearing any headgear! Mary Stewart (born 1888) is seated third from the left in the front row wearing a white dress and hat. The lady on the extreme right holding the wee boy is Margaret Stewart (Mary Stewart's sister), born 1886.

A cart of hay ready to be unloaded onto the large haystack, with Miss McKelvie (Woodburn) and two boarded out girls, Sarah Kelly and Mary Hill, both believed to have come from Port Glasgow. John McIntyre leads the horse, and Sandy Thomson holds the hay rake.

On 4 October 1911 the steamship *Princess Patricia* went aground at the Dippin rocks. Initially she was holed below the water line and having been patched by a salvage team was pumped out. After several unsuccessful attempts to pull her off, salvage operations were suspended on 27 October. Storms then drove her further onto the rocks and her back was broken. She was abandoned as a total wreck and salvaged for scrap over subsequent months. She had been carrying a general cargo.

These nine men were engaged in the salvage operations. Note the winch on the right, which must have been used extensively. Among what was salvaged were sewing machines, although they had no shuttles or needles. At least one local man 'acquired' a machine and took it home. He wrote to the Jones Sewing Machine Company for needles, which started a chain of enquiry and led to two men being taken to court in Rothesay. They were admonished but allowed to keep the sewing machines. Peter MacKenzie, second from the right in the front row, married Jeannie McLennan, Miss McKelvie's niece. He salvaged a bale of cloth with a very colourful pattern which he gave to his sister-in-law, Mrs Ballantyne. The cloth was considered unsuitable for making clothes from because it was so brightly patterned, but Mrs Ballantyne had dresses made from it for her daughters, which led to unfavourable comment from some local people.

Jeannie McLennan (Miss McKelvie's niece) at the spinning wheel.

A picture taken near the pierhead in Whiting Bay in the late 1930s. The village is the third largest on the island after Lamlash and Brodick, and is a typical small coastal resort with boarding houses and small hotels. Whiting Bay is a much quieter place now that the pier no longer exists and there is no steamer traffic.

The golf course in 1910. Three years earlier the course had been extended to eighteen holes and a clubhouse had been built in 1908. This is a most spectacular course high above Whiting Bay, measuring 4,405 yards with a par of 63. Its hills require a bit of energy, but the effort is well worth it for the view. The original course of nine holes was established in 1895, and the first tee was on the site of the current fifth tee.

The Whiting Bay Hotel in 1913.

This shop was established in 1912 and the premises were in use until the business moved to Sandbraes in Whiting Bay itself around 1916. Alexander McKelvie also operated a van which served the south end of the island and Lamlash. Like many other stores, this one also published local postcard views.

The tennis courts in 1925, with the outline of Holy Isle in the background.

The *Glen Sannox* makes her way back to Ardrossan in 1925, via King's Cross, Lamlash and Brodick. This pier, the last to be built on the island, was opened in 1899 and was the longest on the Firth of Clyde. It continued in use until 1962, and was demolished in 1964.

This picture gives an impression of how long the pier was and the walk that passengers had to make from the steamer to shore, which was especially unwelcome if they were carrying holiday luggage. The photograph dates from prior to 1912.

The *Duchess of Argyll* was built in 1906 and was used on the Ardrossan–Arran route from then to 1911. Thereafter, until 1935, she was associated with the service from Gourock to Arran via the Kyles of Bute. This picture also shows the G&SWR's *Glen Sannox* in the background.

A few passengers shelter, while children play, awaiting the arrival of the steamer. The gangway is ready to be hoisted aboard when the steamer docks.

This jetty was used by small rowing boats and those that wanted to do a bit of fishing in the bay. In this picture the steamer *Jupiter* is lying alongside.

A. C. Lennox's Pier Garage at Whiting Bay with assorted hire cars and a Fiat charabanc photographed in the late 1920s.

A Chevrolet charabanc belonging to Jas. Anderson of Whiting Bay crossing the ford at Dougarie in the late 1920s.

As a holiday resort Whiting Bay has much to offer besides golf, bowling and tennis. One of the more spectacular walks leads past the golf course and up the glen of the Ashdale burn. The burn, which when in spate can swell to the size of a river, includes beautiful waterfalls that cascade down from a height of 700 feet. The path on either side of the glen is a well-maintained forestry track that leads through a conifer forest. The trees obscure the view of the falls to some extent, but there are specially constructed viewpoints from which the water can be seen safely.

The Giants Graves, another site of archaeological interest, lie in Glen Ashdale. They are the remains of late Stone Age burial chambers. The site is now within the conifer forest, so the view as shown in this picture is no longer visible.

King's Cross point, between Whiting Bay and Lamlash, is opposite the lighthouse on the south end of Holy Isle. At one time there was a fort there, and a Viking grave mound has also been identified and excavated. The name came about as a result of the tradition of Bruce having visited the island. This was a stopping off point for steamers, and allowed passengers to go ashore between Whiting Bay and Lamlash. They were taken off by ferry boat. Steamers called here regularly until 1923. This picture shows the steamer *Jupiter* in 1912 or earlier.

The ferry boat landing passengers at King's Cross.

King's Cross post office and store was closed on 13 April 1978 on the death of Alan Cook, who had been postmaster for almost 60 years. An interesting feature was the post box to the right of the window, which had a brass flap with the word LETTERS embossed on it.

The main street in Lamlash, 1913. With a population similar to that of Brodick, Lamlash is one of the largest villages on Arran and sits in a sheltered bay overlooked by the Holy Isle. There have always been many hotels and boarding houses. A postcard from Sillars Temperance Hotel, dealing with an enquiry about tariffs in 1911, stated that terms were 42 shillings per week, full board.

Altachorvie Guest House is the home of the Holiday Fellowship in Lamlash. This was originally started in Arran by a group from Conway in North Wales who purchased the house in 1924. The organisation's aims were to provide guided holidays with a Christian-based fellowship, 'to promote healthy enjoyment of leisure, to encourage love of the open air, and provide social and international friendships'. Other centres exist today in Germany, Switzerland, France and Holland. The original house has gradually been extended to accommodate an increasing number of visitors over the years. Some postcards were specially printed for the Holiday Fellowship, and views of other parts of Arran, such as one of Corrie, have the fellowship name on the front of the card.

A 1937 Holiday Fellowship group, all with happy faces and obviously enjoying their stay on Arran. During the Second World War the house was used to accommodate evacuees from Glasgow schools before being requisitioned and taken over by the navy. It became a 'Wrennery', where women serving in the WRNS were stationed.

This row of houses, known as Hamilton Terrace, has a very distinctive character and is still recognisable today. The grocers and provisions shop also housed the post office.

The houses of Hamilton Terrace still overlook the wide village green, which in turn looks over the bay to Holy Isle. A monument was erected in front of the terrace by descendants of those who left for Canada, and is dedicated to the memory of the people uprooted by the Clearances. These people, mainly from Sannox, sailed from Lamlash on 25 April 1829 on the brig *Caledonia*. The village green was once an area where fishermen dried their nets.

Little has changed since this picture of Lamlash was taken *c*.1907. The parish church of Kilbride was built by the 12th Duke of Hamilton and was presented to the village in 1884.

This 1899 photograph shows the pierhead at Lamlash. The pier was busy not only with the steamer service, but with the arrival and departure of tenders belonging to the warships of the Channel Fleet, which used the bay as a safe anchorage. A postcard written from 50 Mess, HMS *Neptune*, Lamlash, thanks 'Daisy' for the books, and also adds that the ship will be in Greenock the following week, so the crew shall have a chance to look round 'Glascow'. It is signed 'Jack xxxx'.

A new pier was built at Lamlash in 1884 and was demolished between 1950 and 1954 when steamers ceased calling at it. The distinctive square clock tower has survived and remains a significant landmark on the Lamlash seafront. The bowling green was situated directly beside the access road to the pier.

A. C. Lennox of Whiting Bay operated this 14 seat Chevrolet between Lamlash and Brodick in the late 1920s. The proprietor himself – A. C. Lennox – is standing (with bow tie) alongside.

Lamlash today is the administrative, health and education centre for the island, with much to offer both residents and visitors alike. Yachting, boating and fishing, combined with a yacht club, boatyard and slipway and the headquarters of the inshore lifeboat, provide interesting viewing along the seafront. The Isle of Arran War Memorial Hospital, overlooking the bay, was opened in 1922 in memory of those who gave their lives during the First World War. It came under the control of the National Health Service in 1948, and has proved to be an invaluable asset to the island. Arran High School is based in Lamlash and provides secondary education for pupils from all over the island.

In 1892 the eighteen hole golf course at Lamlash was the first to open on the island. During the First World War personnel from the fleet were given the courtesy of the course when visiting Lamlash Bay. In return the navy presented trophies to the club, which are still played for in local competitions.

As one approaches Lamlash from Brodick a fine view of the Holy Isle is revealed across Lamlash Bay. The golf course lies to the left of the road.

The agricultural show still held annually at Lamlash draws entries of cattle, sheep and horses from all over the island. Here the champion Ayrshire dairy cow is being paraded by Colin Currie of Balmichael farm in August 1963.

In the early days of the steamboats, Lamlash was the preferred port because of its deep bay and substantial stone pier, seen in this photograph.

The 18-knot *Duchess of Hamilton* started sailing on the new Caledonian Steam Packet Ardrossan to Arran service on 30 May 1890. In 1915 she was withdrawn and transferred to the navy to act as a minesweeper. She was lost the same year.

The *Marchioness of Graham* was on the Ardrossan–Arran run between 1936 and 1958. She was then sold to Greece and renamed *Hellas*. She also ran on excursion routes from Ayr between 1947 and 1953, as well as helping out the *Glen Sannox* on the Ardrossan–Brodick route.

TS *Glen Sannox* replaced the first steamship of that name in 1925, and was a turbine ship of the same design as the *Duchess of Argyll*. She was the main Brodick ferry, and during the war operated from Fairlie, being relieved from time to time by the *Marchioness of Graham*. She carried goods as well as passengers, with luggage and cars being loaded on to the after deck by means of planks from the pier. In 1957 a new purpose-built car ferry, called *Glen Sannox*, took over. Its first day of operation was 29 June.

FURTHER READING

The books listed below were used by the author during his research. None of them are available from Stenlake Publishing. Those interested in finding out more are advised to contact their local bookshop or reference library.

The Book of Arran, Vols. I & II, first published by The Arran Society of Glasgow, 1914, reprinted by Kilbrannan Publishing Ltd., Brodick, 1982.
Brodick Old and New, James C. Inglis.
Arran Place Names, Rev. Alexander Cameron, 1890.
Place Names of Arran, Ronald Currie, 1908.
The Isle of Arran, Robert McLellan, 1970.
All About Arran, R. Angus Downie, 1933.
Tramping in Arran, Tom S. Hall, 1928.
Discovering Arran, Alastair Gemmell, 1990.
The Isle of Arran, Robert McLellan, 1995.
Pictorial History of Arran, Andrew Boyle, 1994.
History of the Villages of Isle of Arran, SWRI Arran Federation, 1983.
Clyde Piers, Ian McCrorie, 1982.
Clyde Pleasure Steamers, Ian McCrorie, 1986.
The Sea Routes to Arran, Ian McCrorie, 1993.
Clyde Shipwrecks, Peter Moir and Ian Crawford, 1988.
Arran Shipwrecks, Donald Johnston, 1994.
Arran Bus Book, Mitchell-Luker, 1983.
Islands Postal History Series No. 5, Arran & Cumbrae, James A. Mackay, 1978.

Bearing a Whiting Bay postmark dated 1 September 1919, this is rather an unusual subject for a holiday postcard. It has an unusual delivery address, too: 27 Amhurst Road, Pennycomequick, Plymouth, England. Despite its oddity, the picture provides an interesting insight into how Arran roads were built and maintained. Roadside quarries such as this one are still visible today, especially on winding corners and steep hillsides, and it was these which provided the basic road metal. After 1807, with the introduction of wheeled vehicles to the island, better roads were required. In 1817 the String road was planned by Thomas Telford and built by a contractor. The Ross road was built in 1821, extending from the Parliamentary road between Brodick and Lamlash. By 1843, when the road from Sannox to Lochranza was completed, the various stretches of road round the island had been joined up. The card shows Mick Cannon and his mate beside the quarry. There was no mechanisation, and working with hammer, pick and shovel must have been very hard.

Back cover, upper The firm of Alexander Wooley and Son was established at Invercloy in the 1880s, and Wooley's bakery is still in much the same place today. Alexander Wooley initially owned a cottage, then bought an adjoining property and developed a thriving grocery, bakery and tea shop. Described as a 'Superior Tearoom', the latter was upstairs above the shop and opened in 1902. The family lived to the right above the shop, and the bakery was at the back of the premises. The present bakery shop is to the left of the shop frontage shown here, situated in what was originally the office.
Back cover, lower: A 1900s scene outside Whiting Bay Hotel.

ISBN 9781840336351
9 781840 336351
£20.00
Stenlake Publishing
www.stenlake.co.uk